EVOLUTION

This is an ocean sunfish, one of the largest fish in the sea. The females breed once a year and release 300 million eggs into the water. Most of the baby sunfish will die, but a few make it to adulthood. They start out at a length of just 2.5mm and have to get 60 million times bigger to be fully grown!

Evolution is the process by which living things can change gradually. Over millions of years, many tiny changes add up to some big differences. Evolution is why there are so many different species living on Earth. Some species are obviously more closely related than others. In 1859, Charles Darwin said that related species had evolved from the same ancestor in the past. He explained how evolution could do that with a process called natural selection.

Animals in a species may look the same, but they all have a unique set of variations. These differences make some animals 'fitter' than others. The fitter ones are better at surviving in wild conditions than others. Darwin said that nature 'selects' these fit animals; they have many children, while the unfit ones die off. Over time, the characteristics that make an animal fit become more common, and eventually every member of the species has it — the species has evolved a tiny bit.

Evolution is not only driven by survival. The reason why animals struggle and compete to survive is so they can reproduce.

Once they have reproduced, animal parents have evolved different ways of making sure their offspring survive long enough so they, in turn, can reproduce themselves. Some animals do this by producing huge numbers of offspring, perhaps millions of them. Even though most of them will die, at least a few are sure to make it to adulthood. Most of the creatures in this book have just a few young and take very good care of them in different ways. Let's take a look at some of nature's best parents!

CHEETAH

NATURE'S BEST
PARENTS

HOW ANIMALS
RAISE, PROTECT
AND FEED
THEIR YOUNG

TOM JACKSON

{CONTENTS}

CHEETAH... 4

MEERKAT.. 6

SILVERED LEAF MONKEY................. 8

SURINAME TOAD 9

SOCKEYE SALMON 10

EMPEROR PENGUIN 12

GREY WHALE 14

SEAHORSE 15

SCORPION..................................... 16

RED KANGAROO............................ 18

AFRICAN ELEPHANT...................... 20

ORANG-UTAN.............................. 21

FLAMINGO.................................... 22

TERMITE QUEEN........................... 24

CROCODILES................................ 26

DUNG BEETLE.............................. 28

PACIFIC OCTOPUS....................... 29

GLOSSARY.................................... 30

FURTHER INFORMATION.............. 31

INDEX.. 32

Mother cheetahs have to keep their babies on the move. The newborn cubs are left snoozing in a quiet spot while their mother goes hunting during the day. The den is perfectly safe for a day or two, but will begin to smell of cheetah as time goes on – and that might attract hungry lions or hyenas. So, the mother moves her family regularly, gently holding each cub in her mouth as she pads off to a safer location.

MEERKAT

Meerkat families live in underground dens in the African desert. They are safe underground, but being at the surface is much more dangerous. When most of the adults go off to find food, one will stand guard over the young, or kits. Returning hunters often bring a treat back for the kits.

Meerkats live in groups, called a clan, or a mob. Most mobs have about 20 meerkats living in them, but some are twice this big. Each mob is ruled by an alpha pair. This is a chief male and female who are the only ones who have babies each year. If another member of the mob has young, the alphas may kill the babies. The chiefs want every member of their gang to work together raising their young — not anyone else's.

EVOLUTION SOLUTION

Meerkats live in a dry habitat where food is spread out over a large area. Finding enough food takes a long time and it is very risky. Meerkats have evolved to work together so they can take it in turns to look for food, watch out for danger and look after the young.

The older meerkats bring the young some food, such as this tasty scorpion.

When guarding the young, the adult meerkat stands on its back legs, so it can see as far as possible.

The kits are born underground in the cosy den and are only strong enough to come to the surface when they are about three weeks old. The adults take it in turns to guard the kits. Any female mob member can feed them milk, even though she is not their parent.

The kits learn to catch prey by watching the adults. The adults bring them scorpions to practise on. The first lesson is with a dead scorpion; the second is with a live one, but the stinger has been bitten off. The final lesson is with a fully armed scorpion. By the time a kit is three months old, it is ready to hunt for itself.

FACTS AND FIGURES

Scientific name....... Suricata suricatta
Location.................. South-west Africa
Habitat............................Semi-desert
Size...35–50cm
Food........... Insects, scorpions, reptiles
Lifespan................................. 7 years
Young.................. 3 kits born each year

Meerkats have six alarm calls. Three of them warn of an attack from the air, and the other three warn of attack from on land. Each call also indicates how near the danger is.

SILVERED LEAF MONKEY

Silvered leaf monkeys live in large groups ruled by one chief male, who has children with many females. The females work as a team to look after all the young, which are easy to spot among the leaves.

At night, silvered leaf monkeys huddle together in a tree to sleep. During the day, smaller groups go off to look for food. Females with babies are in charge of these smaller groups, and all the other monkeys help to carry and suckle the young. A mother can produce milk for one year after giving birth. However, the babies need milk for 18 months. This means older children are fed by females who still have young babies.

The orange babies need to be carried through the forest.

EVOLUTION SOLUTION

Most animals are able to reproduce for their whole lives. However, female silvered leaf monkeys stay alive for many years after they are able to have children. These older monkeys help look after their grandchildren, which ensures the group has healthy offspring that are cared for.

FACTS AND FIGURES

Scientific name............Trachypithecus cristatus

Location.......................Southeast Asia

Habitat................................Rainforests

Size..45–60cm

Food..Leaves

Lifespan...................................30 years

Young.........................Single babies born throughout the year

The adult monkeys are black, but the babies are born with bright orange fur and pale white faces. This is a signal to older monkeys that the baby needs constant care. By the age of five months, the young monkey has turned black and is able to look after itself a bit more.

SURINAME TOAD

Most frogs and toads lay eggs in water. They hatch into tadpoles who must fend for themselves. However, the Suriname toad takes better care of its babies.

Suriname toads spend their whole lives in water. They have very flat bodies which helps them burrow into the riverbed. They have huge webs on their back feet, but the forelegs have long, sensitive toes for feeling for worms and fish to eat in the gloomy waters.

After mating, the male sweeps the eggs on to his mate's back, where they are glued stuck. The eggs become embedded in the mother's back and develop there for three months. When they hatch through the mother's skin, it is not tadpoles that emerge, but tiny toadlets.

EVOLUTION SOLUTION

Protecting the eggs and the developing young under the mother's thick skin ensures that most young, if not all, will grow into toads. Most frogs and toads lay hundreds of eggs and nearly all of them are eaten before they hatch or when they are still tadpoles.

FACTS AND FIGURES

Scientific name.........................Pipa pipa
Location..............................South America
Habitat................................Deep riverbed
Size..18cm
Food....................Fish and invertebrates
Lifespan...................................8 years
Young..........................Up to 100 toadlets

Toadlets emerge from holes in the mother's back.

SOCKEYE SALMON

Sockeye salmon parents have to work very hard to create their offspring. So hard, that they will die from exhaustion once they have succeeded. Like all species of salmon, the sockeye changes habitat throughout its life. It hatches from an egg in a mountain river, becomes fully grown in the ocean far downstream, and then must swim all the way back again to spawn.

{ **AMAZING FEATURES** }
A sockeye salmon's spawning ground may be 2,100m above sea level.

This salmon is attempting to leap over a waterfall as it heads upstream. It can take dozens of attempts and many fish die trying.

FACTS AND FIGURES

Scientific name.... Oncorhynchus nerka
Location........................ Northern Pacific
Habitat............. Rivers, lakes and ocean
Size...................................... 60–80cm
Foo............................. Plankton, shrimps
Lifespan... 5 years
Young................... Hundreds of eggs laid in shallow freshwater

Young salmon spend one or two years feeding in lakes or rivers. When they are big enough, the fish swim with the current downstream to the ocean. They do not stray too far from the shore, but there is more food for them in the deep ocean water. The salmon spend two or three years at sea, growing to full size. At this time the fish are silvering blue in colour, but as they reach full maturity and get ready to mate, they turn red.

Some sockeyes don't migrate to the ocean. Instead, they spend their lives in lakes or large rivers.

The adult fish will spawn in the same water where they hatched themselves. The bodies of migrating fish develop powerful muscles for the tough swim against the current. The journey, which can be as long as 1,500km, can take eight months, during which time the fish will not feed at all.

Once at the spawning grounds, the females dig little hollows in the gravel riverbed. They lay eggs in these nests, known as redds. The females protect their redds for as long as possible. Within a week or two, the adults' energy stores run out and they die. The hundreds of dead fish are rich pickings for bears and eagles.

EVOLUTION SOLUTION

The salmon's life of long-distant travel evolved as the fish spread out to find new sources of food. The ocean contains much more food than the rivers, so a much larger population of salmon can survive there. However, the ancestors of salmon lived in freshwater, and baby salmon, or fry, cannot survive in seawater. Therefore, their parents must swim back inland to lay eggs.

EMPEROR PENGUIN

To raise their chick, emperor penguin parents must brave the harshest winter on Earth and travel hundreds of kilometres over the Antarctic ice.

Penguins spend the summer hunting for fish in the sea. In autumn, they climb on to the ice that freezes over the ocean and move to a breeding ground. It takes many days and nights to reach this area, which is sheltered from the wind.

Soon after the penguins arrive, the Sun sets for the Antarctic winter — it will not come up again for nearly three months! Each female lays one big egg, and in the dark she quickly moves it on top of her mate's feet. He keeps it warm under a flap of feathery skin called the brood pouch. The females then head back to sea to feed, but the males stay on the ice throughout the winter. The temperature drops to –60°C and the wind whistles along at 200 km/h! The egg is safe on the dad's feet, but he must huddle together with his neighbours to stay warm.

After the Sun rises again over two months later, the egg hatches. The scrawny chick

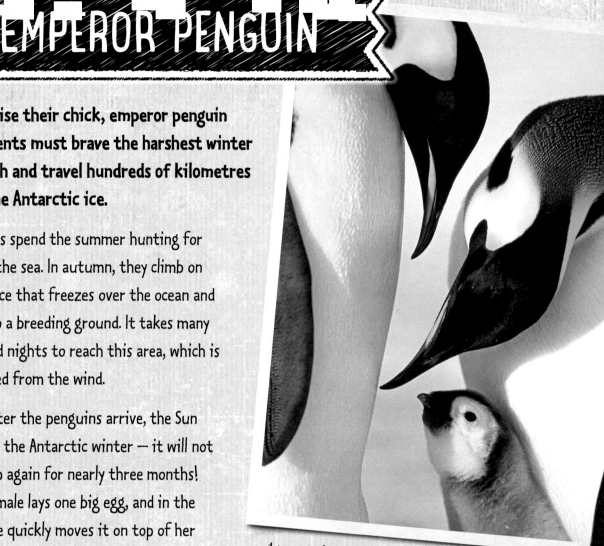

A penguin family finds each other in the crowd by using a unique squawking call.

FACTS AND FIGURES

Scientific name.. Aptenodytes forsteri
Location.................................... Antarctica
Habitat................................Oceans and ice
Size... 115cm tall
Food... Fish
Lifespan...........................Up to 20 years
Young..............1 chick hatches each year

stays inside the brood pouch to keep warm. Its father's stomach is empty, but he feeds his chick an oily liquid made in his throat.

Within a few days, the females return, and the fathers hand over the chicks to their mothers. The females are full of food and start to feed their chicks. The males have lost half their body weight, so hurry to the sea to feed. For the next five months, the mum and dad take it in turns to hunt for fish and care for the chick.

Older chicks huddle together for warmth and are sheltered by a ring of adults.

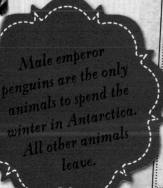

Male emperor penguins are the only animals to spend the winter in Antarctica. All other animals leave.

EVOLUTION SOLUTION

The seas around Antarctica have plenty of fish for the penguins to eat, but like all birds, penguins must lay their eggs out of the water. There is nowhere else for emperor penguins to go but the ice, and there is nothing to eat there. So, the species has evolved a system where the parents take it in turns to look after their egg and chick while the other one hunts for food. The penguins have evolved to be big so they can store a lot of fat.

GREY WHALE

The calf is already 4m long at birth. It survives on its mother's milk for its first journey to the northern feeding grounds.

During the migration, the whales swim 24 hours a day at 8km/h.

Grey whales spend the summer feeding in the cold waters of the northern ocean. As winter approaches, they swim south, making a 10,000km journey in less than three months to reach warm waters where it is best for their babies to be born.

The first whales to swim south every year are the pregnant females. They head for quiet bays with shallow water where it is less likely that killer whales or sharks will attack the newborn calf.

Calves are born underwater, and the mother helps them swim up to the surface for their first breath of air. The mother and child rest for a few weeks in the warm water; then it is time for both to make the long swim north in search of rich feeding grounds.

EVOLUTION SOLUTION

The grey whale's breeding system has evolved to be in time with its migration. Pregnant mothers migrate to a warm place to give birth. The calf has no layer of fat at birth, so needs to be in warm waters. The other whales make the same journey to mate. The females will return a year later to give birth.

FACTS AND FIGURES

Scientific name.... Eschrichtius robustus
Location................................North Pacific
Habitat.......................................Oceans
Size.. 15m
Food...................................Crustaceans
Lifespan................................. 60 years
Young........ 1 calf born every two years

SEAHORSE

Many male animals help to look after their offspring. However, the seahorse is the only animal in the world where the male gives birth to his young!

Once the eggs have hatched inside him, the male releases the baby fish, which then swim away.

FACTS AND FIGURES

Scientific name	Hippocampus
Location	Worldwide
Habitat	Seas and oceans
Size	2–30cm
Food	Plankton
Lifespan	3–5 years
Young	20–2,000 eggs laid in male's pouch

While the male is brooding the eggs, the female comes to check on him every day.

Seahorses are tube-shaped fish that cling to seaweeds in shallow seawater. They are not very strong swimmers, and just suck up food from the water with their trumpet-shaped snouts. Seahorse mates perform a long courtship dance that lasts for several hours.

The female's body is swollen with eggs, and she lays them inside a pouch on the male's tummy. The male then fertilises the eggs. His pouch supplies the eggs with oxygen and nutrients, and keeps them safe until they hatch two weeks later.

EVOLUTION SOLUTION

Many fish breed using external fertilisation. This means the female lays her eggs first and the male then fertilises them with sperm. As the female swims off first, it is often the male fish who is left to look after the eggs. Some males guard the nest or carry the eggs in their mouths. The seahorses have simply evolved a system where the male carries the eggs in a protective pouch.

SCORPION

The growing babies take up a lot of room inside the female. Her body becomes very stretched.

Scorpions do not lay eggs. Instead, the baby scorpions grow inside their mother. She feeds them as they develop and then gives birth to them. That may not sound that unusual — it is what most mammal mothers do — but it is very rare for this kind of animal.

A scorpion is very well armed, with powerful pincers and a pointed stinger. With all these weapons, scorpions are very quick to attack. As a result, when searching for a mate, a male approaches a female cautiously. He holds her pincers so she cannot nip him — she will still threaten him with her stinger. Then, the male walks backwards leading his mate along in a kind of dance.

The male may sting his mate to make her less aggressive towards him.

FACTS AND FIGURES

Scientific name...................... Scorpiones
Location................................ Worldwide
Habitat.................... Deserts and jungles
Size.. 1–20cm
Food.................... Insects, frogs, lizards
Lifespan.......................... Up to 10 years
Young......................... About 8 scorplings

The male is looking for a flat bit of ground. When he finds one, he drops a bag of sperm and pulls the female over it so the sperm goes inside her body to mix with her eggs. Then, the male runs away as quickly as possible!

The eggs hatch inside the female a few days later, but the babies stay inside the ovary (egg pouch). They get food from a milk-like liquid that arrives through the ovary wall from the mother's stomach. The babies, or scorplings, live in the pouch for several weeks while they grow.

When they are finally born, the scorplings have pincers and working stingers, but they still need protection from their mother. They ride around on her back, taking nibbles of the food she catches. Only when they have developed a tough exoskeleton, several weeks, or even month later, do the scorplings begin to go off on their own.

EVOLUTION SOLUTION

Scorpion eggs are very small, and when the scorplings hatch they are too tiny to hunt and defend themselves. Scorpions have evolved to start out by growing inside their mother because this is a way for them to grow in a protected environment before they have to fend for themselves.

The newborn scorpions stay on their mother's back until their skin gets harder.

RED KANGAROO

Female kangaroos are famous for carrying their babies — known as joeys — in a pouch. A kangaroo joey is born after just 33 days of developing inside its mother; a human baby takes 280! The pouch gives the joey a place to complete its development.

Kangaroos belong to a small group of mammals called marsupials. Nearly all other mammals are placental mammals. This means the young develop inside their mothers. They spend a long time growing there and are supplied with food and oxygen through an organ called the placenta. Kangaroos do not have placentas. Instead, a joey gets its nutrients from the milk in its mum's pouch. So to access it, the joey needs to be born.

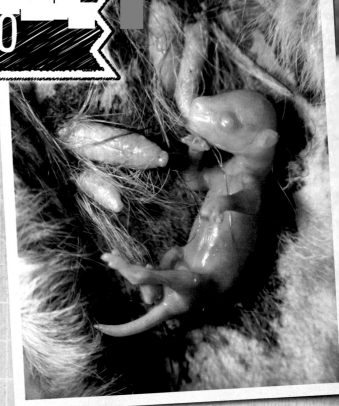

The joey can suck milk and breathe at the same time!

The pouch stretches to hold the joey, although the baby's long feet don't quite fit!

EVOLUTION SOLUTION

Most mammal babies start growing inside their mothers before being born. Having a baby inside the body causes a problem: the mother's immune system is built to destroy anything that is not part of the body, including a baby. So placental mammals have a barrier that keeps apart the blood of the mother and the baby's blood. Marsupial babies are born before the immune system can attack them, and then complete their development outside the mother's body.

FACTS AND FIGURES

Scientific name............ Macropus rufus
Location.. Australia
Habitat.................................Grasslands
Size.. 1.3–2.5m
Food........................Grass and leaves
Lifespan.................................... 18 years
Young......................1 or 2 joeys per year

When a joey is born it looks more like a worm than a kangaroo. It has no back legs and its front legs are long claws, which it uses to haul itself from the birth canal to the pouch. Once in the pouch, the joey finds a teat and begins to drink milk. It is suckled continuously for the next 70 days. After that, it is strong enough to move around inside the pouch, and at the age of six months it goes for short hops around outside.

At this point, a younger joey may arrive in the pouch. There is room for both. When it is one year old, a joey stops drinking milk. It leaves the pouch for good and eats grass.

When joeys of different ages are in the same pouch, they are supplied with different kinds of milk.

As it approaches its first birthday, the joey has become a bit big for the pouch.

AMAZING FEATURES
A joey weighs just 1g at birth, yet it crawls to its mum's pouch within three minutes.

AFRICAN ELEPHANT

It takes almost two years for a baby elephant to develop inside its mother. When it is born, it already weighs twice as much as an adult woman. Even though it is so big, it still needs looking after, and the entire elephant family helps out.

When a new baby, or calf, is born, the elephant family gathers round it to see their new member. They stroke it with their trunks and make deep, soothing sounds. To start with, the mother elephant is very protective of her calf, but soon the other females in the group begin to help out. Mostly, these are young females who have not had their own young yet like to babysit.

The calf needs help with everything to start with. It is unsteady on its feet and often trips over its own trunk. But it learns fast and by the age of one it can walk, run and feed itself. However, it will still drink its mother's milk for another year or two.

EVOLUTION SOLUTION

The elephant family system has evolved because it takes calves 12 years to grow into adults. In that time, mothers need help with raising their young. Also, the babysitters that help out learn how to be a good mother for when they have a baby of their own.

FACTS AND FIGURES

Scientific name...... Loxodonta africana
Location... Africa
Habitat...................... Grasslands, jungles
Size.. 2.5–4m tall
Food...................................... Leaves, wood
Lifespan.. 70 years
Young....... 1 calf born every four years

The calf does not leave its mother's side for the first three months of its life.

ORANG-UTAN

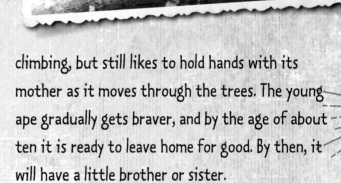

Orang-utans have the the longest childhood of any animal — if we don't count humans! A female orang-utan only has one baby every nine years. This is the longest gap between brothers and sisters of any animal in the world. Even whales or elephants have their children faster than this.

Unlike the other great apes, orang-utans live alone. This means the mothers do all the childcare by themselves. They also stay high in the trees most of the time, which makes bringing up babies even harder. A newborn does not let go of its mother at all for the first four months of its life. If it did, it would fall to the ground. By the age of two, the young is better at

The orang-utan has thumbs on its feet as well as on its hands.

climbing, but still likes to hold hands with its mother as it moves through the trees. The young ape gradually gets braver, and by the age of about ten it is ready to leave home for good. By then, it will have a little brother or sister.

FACTS AND FIGURES

Scientific name	Pongo
Location	Sumatra and Borneo
Habitat	Rainforests
Size	125–175cm
Food	Leaves, fruits, insects, eggs, honey
Lifespan	30 years
Young	1 infant born every nine years

EVOLUTION SOLUTION

Orang-utans are very intelligent. They have to be, to survive in a complex place like a forest. The apes can remember where to find many different kinds of food in their habitat, and they also know what time of year to look for it. Then they need to figure out how to get there safely. An orang-utan baby is not with this knowledge. It has to it learn from its mother, which takes time. This is why orang-utans have evolved to grow up so slowly.

FLAMINGO

Flamingoes are tall wading birds that live in shallow water. They gather in huge flocks to stay safe from any attacks. However, finding somewhere to raise a chick in such a big crowd is hard work.

Once the crèche is big enough, the flamingo parents leave their chicks to look after themselves.

HEAD-DOWN
Flamingos are the only birds to feed with their heads upside down.

FACTS AND FIGURES

Scientific name................. Phoeniconaias

Location....... North and South America. Africa and Asia

Habitat........... Salt lakes and seashores

Size..................................... 90 to 150cm

Food...................... Shrimps and plankton

Lifespan..................................... 20 years

Young.................... 1 egg laid a year

Flamingoes live in mudflats by the sea or in lakes. Their beaks have a comb-like sieving system that lets them suck out algae and shrimps that live in the mud.

The mud is covered in shallow water much of the year, and this causes a problem when it is time to lay an egg. Eggs must be kept dry, so air can get through the shell to the chick growing inside. So, flamingo mates work together to build a mud platform up to 30cm above the water. The female lays a single egg on top of the mound, and the pair work together to stop it falling into the water. They may also have to fight off other birds who want to steal the mound for their own egg.

When the egg hatches, the chick stays on the mound out of the water, being fed by both parents. In its second week, the chick climbs down into the muddy water. The chicks gather together for safety in a little group called a crèche. As the chicks get older, their crèche will merge with others nearby, until there are thousands of chicks in one big flock.

Young chicks are fed an oily liquid, called 'crop milk', which comes from their parents' stomachs.

The parents make sure the egg does not fall off the mound. If it did, it would be very difficult to rescue it from the water.

EVOLUTION SOLUTION

Flamingoes have evolved a unique feeding system which allows them to sift bacteria and shrimps from soft mud. This kind of food would make most other animals sick, so the flamingoes have plenty of food available in the mudflat habitat. However, raising a chick on a mudflat is a difficult job, which is why the birds have evolved their mud-nest system to protect the eggs and chicks.

TERMITE QUEEN

This big blob is a queen termite. She does nothing all day but lay eggs. She can produce up to 30,000 a day. The eggs are looked after by worker termites, which are also the queen's offspring. The workers keep the queen clean and feed her. A queen, such as this this, could live for 25 years.

CROCODILES

Crocodiles are among the most powerful predators on the planet. They have been hunting and killing in the world's rivers for at least 200 million years. However, crocodile parents spend a lot of time caring for their young and will even use their fearsome, toothy mouths to keep their babies safe.

Hatching baby crocodiles use a spike on their snouts, called an egg tooth, to break the egg shell. As soon as the head is through, the egg tooth falls off.

The crocodile has one of the strongest bites in the animals kingdom, but a crocodile mother is able to carry her young without harming them.

Crocodiles and alligators are water animals. They specialise in lurking in shallow water beside a river bank and grabbing prey that come down to the water's edge to drink. Males attract mates by bellowing loudly in the water. After mating, the females must come on to land to lay their eggs.

FACTS AND FIGURES

Scientific name.......... Crocodylomorpha
Location.................................... Worldwide
Habitat...................... Rivers and oceans
Size... 1.5–6m
Food....... Fish, birds, mammals, reptiles
Lifespan........................... Up to 70 years
Young................... 30 eggs laid in nest

While a few crocodile species simply bury their eggs, most put them in a nest made from dried grass and mud. The grass begins to rot, producing a little heat that keeps the nest warm. The female stays close to the nest to prevent lizards and other predators from stealing the eggs.

When it is time to hatch, the young crocodiles give out high-pitched calls from inside the egg. These are a signal to the mother to dig the eggs out of the nest. The babies then crack their way out of the eggs. The babies are ready to hunt for themselves, with tiny, razor-sharp teeth. However, their mother usually gives them a lift to the water inside her huge mouth. She will then guard her gaggle of young for several weeks as they look for food in the water. One of the biggest dangers for the babies is being eaten by other crocodiles!

EVOLUTION SOLUTION

Whether a crocodile egg grows into a male or female baby depends on the nest temperature. If the nest is cool or warm, the eggs will be female. If the temperature is in between, about 32°C, they will mostly be male. No one knows why crocodiles have evolved this system. One suggestion is that more female babies will hatch early in the breeding season when it is bit cooler, and so be ready to breed sooner.

A Nile crocodile's bite is seven times more powerful than that of a great white shark.

DUNG BEETLE

The ancient Egyptians believed the Sun was rolled across the sky each day by a dung beetle god, called Khepri.

As its name may suggest, the dung beetle eats the poo of larger animals. They also use a ball of dung as a nursery for their young!

A dung beetle sniffs out dung using smell detectors on its antennae. Once it catches the right whiff, it flies over to the dollop of dung and uses its flattened front legs to carve out a chunk of poo. Working with its mate, it molds that into a ball and rolls it away. Next, the beetles dig a hole to bury the dung.

Once the ball is buried, the female lays an egg next to it, and fills in the hole. The egg hatches into a grub which burrows into the dung and eats its way out from the inside!

The beetle pushes the ball with its long back legs – and so has to do a handstand and walk backwards!

A young dung beetle emerges from a dung ball.

EVOLUTION SOLUTION

Plant foods are hard to digest, and the dung of a large herbivore, like a cow, still contains half of the original nutrients. Dung beetles have evolved to survive on dung as a source of food that is easy to digest and never in short supply.

FACTS AND FIGURES

Scientific name.................. Scarabaeidae
Location.................................... Worldwide
Habitat.......................Grasslands, jungles
Size... 1–3cm
Food.. Dung
Lifespan...................................... 3 years
Young.................... 1 grub per dung ball

28

PACIFIC OCTOPUS

The giant Pacific octopus is the world's biggest octopus, growing to 10m across with is tentacles outstretched. This giant can have 100,000 young and will lay down its life for them all.

The giant Pacific octopus breeds when it is about five years old — earlier if it lives in warmer water with more food. During mating, the male octopus transfers a packet of sperm to the female. The packet can be 1m long! The female uses the sperm to fertilise thousands of eggs, and she then lays them inside her den. The eggs take six months to develop, and the female never leaves them, not even to feed. She pumps fresh water over the eggs to keep them clean and healthy. By the time the babies hatch, the mother has starved herself to death.

FACTS AND FIGURES

Scientific name.. Enteroctopus dofleini
Location............................. North Pacific
Habitat............................... Deep seabed
Size.. 4–10m
Food..................fish, lobsters, shrimps
Lifespan.................................. 4–5 years
Young............. Up to 100,000 eggs laid

EVOLUTION SOLUTION

A female octopus only gets one chance to be a parent, and she devotes all her energy to it. This system evolved so the octopus can produce many thousands of eggs all at once. Her care then ensures that the eggs are safe and healthy, which makes it more likely that many of them will survive.

The eggs hang in clusters from the roof of their mother's den.

GLOSSARY

Antarctica The continent that surrounds the South Pole. The temperature in Antarctica is nearly always below freezing and almost all the land is covered in deep layers of ice.

alpha The first letter in the Greek alphabet; alpha is often used to describe the main animal in a group.

antennae Sometimes known as feelers, antennae are leg-like structures on the heads of many animals. As well as feeling, antennae are often used for detecting smells.

evolution The process by which animals, plants and other life forms change gradually to adapt to changes in their environment.

female The sex that produces eggs and gives birth to babies.

fertilisation When a sperm and egg from two parents combine to make the first cell of a new offspring. That cell will grow into a baby animal.

habitat The kind of environment that an animal lives in. Each species has evolved to survive in its particular habitat.

male The sex that produces sperm and in almost all cases, does not give birth.

mammal A type of animal that grows hairs on its body and feeds its young milk.

migration A journey made by an animal every year. The migration is always a round trip, so the animal arrives back where it started. The animal migrates to find food, water and a good place to raise young.

natural selection The process by which evolution works. Natural selection allows individuals that are good at surviving to increase in number, while those that are less able to compete go down in number.

nutrients The chemicals that a living body needs to survive.

oxygen The gas that animals breathe from the air or filter from water. Oxygen is used by the body to release energy from food.

predator An animal that hunts and kills other animals for food.

prey An animal that is hunted and killed by a predator.

species A group of animals that share many characteristics. The main common feature is that members of a species can breed with each other. Members of different species cannot produce young successfully.

sperm A sex cell produced by males. Sperms are built to travel to a female egg and fertilise it.

FURTHER INFORMATION

BOOKS

THE WORLD IN INFOGRAPHICS: Animal Kingdom,
by Jon Richards and Ed Simkins (Wayland, 2014)

ANIMAL FAMILIES [SERIES],
by Tim Harris (Wayland, 2014)

WHAT IS EVOLUTION?,
by Louise Spilsbury (Wayland, 2015)

WEBSITES

www.zsl.org/kids

The kids' section of the Zoological Society of London's website is packed with animal information, games and activities, as well as the latest scientific studies.

www.ngkids.co.uk

Animal-related facts, pictures and games from the kids' section of the National Geographic website.

www.nhm.ac.uk/kids-only

The Natural History Museum website is filled with games, facts and information on the world of animals.

INDEX

Africa 6, 7, 20, 22
African elephant 20
alligator 26
Antarctica 12, 13
ape 21
Asia 8, 22
Australia 19

bird 12–13, 22–23, 26
Borneo 21

calf 14, 20
cheetah 4–5
chick 12, 13, 22, 23
crocodile 26–27
crustacean 14
cub 5

desert 6, 7, 16
dung beetle 28

emperor penguin 12–13

evolution 3
external fertilisation 15

fish 3, 9, 10–11, 12, 13, 15, 26, 29
flamingo 22–23
frog 7, 9, 16
fry 11

grassland 19, 20, 28
grey whale 14

hyena 5

infant 21
insect 7, 16, 21
invertebrate 9

joey 19
jungle 16, 20, 28
kit 6, 7

lake 10, 11
lion 5
lizard 16, 27
lobster 29

mammal 16, 18, 26
marsupial 18
meerkat 6–7
migration 11, 14

natural selection 3
Nile crocodile 27
North America 22

ocean 3, 10, 11, 12, 14, 26
offspring 3, 8, 10, 15, 24
orang-utan 21

Pacific 10, 14, 29
Pacific octopus 29
plankton 10, 15, 22

rainforest 8, 21
red kangaroo 18–19
reptile 7, 26
river 9, 10, 11, 26

scorpion 6, 7, 16–17
scorpling 16–17
seahorse 15
seashore 22
shrimp 10, 22, 23, 29
silvered leaf monkey 8
sockeye salmon 10–11
South America 9, 22
spawn 10, 11
species 3, 10, 13, 27
Sumatra 21
Suriname toad 9

termite queen 24–25
toad 9

variation 3

First published in 2015 by Wayland
Copyright © Wayland, 2015

All rights reserved.

Editor: Julia Adams
Designer: Rocket Design

Dewey number: 591.5'63-dc23
ISBN 978 0 7502 8801 9

Printed in China

10 9 8 7 6 5 4 3 2 1

Picture acknowledgements: Cover: © David Tipling/naturepl.com; p. 1,
p. 13 (bottom): © Fred Olivier/naturepl.com; p. 3 © Visuals Unlimited/
naturepl.com; pp. 4–5: © Anup Shah/naturepl.com; p. 6 (centre),
p. 31: © Simon King/naturepl.com; p. 6 (right-hand side): © Solvin
Zankl/naturepl.com; p. 7: © Will Burrard-Lucas/naturepl.com; p. 8:
© Fiona Rogers/naturepl.com; p. 9: © Andrea Florence/ardea.com;
p. 10: © Visuals Unlimited/naturepl.com; p. 11 (top): © Alex Mustard/
naturepl.com; p. 11 (centre): © Michel Roggo/naturepl.com; p. 12: ©
David Tipling/naturepl.com; p. 13 (top): © Fred Olivier/naturepl.com;
p. 14: © James Forte/National Geographic Creative/Corbis; p. 15: ©
Alex Mustard/naturepl.com; p. 16: © Premaphotos/naturepl.com; p.
17 (centre): © Doug Wechsler/naturepl.com; p. 17 (bottom): © Visuals
Unlimited/naturepl.com; p. 18 (top): © Roland Seitre/naturepl.com; p.
18 (bottom): © Dave Watts/naturepl.com; p. 19: © Steven David Miller/
naturepl.com; p. 20: © Tony Heald/naturepl.com; p. 21: © Anup Shah/
naturepl.com; p. 22: © Anup Shah/naturepl.com; p. 23 (top): © Anup
Shah/naturepl.com; p. 23 (bottom): © Denis-Hout/naturepl.com; pp.
24–25: © Shutterstock; p. 26 (top): © Jabruson/naturepl.com; p. 26
(bottom): © Anup Shah/naturepl.com; p. 27: © Jabruson/naturepl.
com; p. 28 (top): © Rolf Nussbaumer/naturepl.com; p. 28 (bottom):
© Nature Production/naturepl.com; p. 29: © Fred Bavendam/Minden
Pictures/Corbis; all images used as graphic elements: Shutterstock.

Wayland, an imprint of Hachette Children's Group
Part of Hodder & Stoughton
Carmelite House
50 Victoria Embankment
London
EC4Y 0DZ

An Hachette UK Company
www.hachette.co.uk
www.hachettechildrens.co.uk

MIX
Paper from
responsible sources
FSC® C104740